KURT WEILL

FRAUENTANZ

Sieben Gedichte des Mittelalters, op. 10 (1923 / 1924)
für Sopran, Flöte, Bratsche, Klarinette, Horn und Fagott
herausgegeben von Jürgen Selk nach dem Text der Kurt Weill Edition

Seven Poems from the Middle Ages, Op. 10 (1923 / 1924)
for soprano, flute, viola, clarinet, horn and bassoon
edited by Jürgen Selk after the text of the Kurt Weill Edition

Partitur
Full Score

UE 33 081 / EA 848 S
ISMN M-008-07706-7
UPC 8-03452-06070-3
ISBN 3-7024-2979-4

Vorwort

Im Gesamtwerk Kurt Weills nimmt Kammermusik einen verhältnismäßig kleinen Teil ein; der Gesamtbestand umfasst das *Streichquartett in h-Moll*, das *I. Streichquartett op. 8*, die *Sonate für Violoncello und Klavier*, den vokal-instrumentalen Liederzyklus *Frauentanz op. 10* sowie die vokal-instrumentale Miniatur *Ick sitze da – un esse Klops*. Diese Werke wurden im Jahre 2004 in einer Kritischen Edition, herausgegeben von Wolfgang Rathert und Jürgen Selk, als Teil der Kurt Weill Edition veröffentlicht (Serie II, Band 1). Die hier vorliegende praktische Ausgabe des Liederzyklus *Frauentanz op. 10* beruht auf dem Text der Kritischen Edition.

Mit Ausnahme des *Klopslieds*, das Weill etwa 1925–1926 komponierte, stammt Weills Kammermusik aus den Jahren 1918–1923. In ihr sind sowohl Weills Entwicklung als junger Komponist reflektiert als auch die äußeren Umstände, die seinen Werdegang beeinflussten, beginnend mit seinem Studium an der Königlich Akademischen Hochschule für Musik in Berlin unter Engelbert Humperdinck (1918–1919), seiner vorübergehenden Tätigkeit als Kapellmeister in Lüdenscheid (1919–1920) und schließlich seinem Studium in Ferruccio Busonis Meisterklasse, beginnend im Jahre 1921.

Schon zwischen dem *Streichquartett in h-Moll* (1918–1919), dessen Fertigstellung im Rahmen von Humperdincks Unterricht erfolgte, und der *Sonate für Violoncello und Klavier* (1919–1920) zeigt sich eine bemerkenswerte stilistische Entwicklung. Während sich das *Streichquartett in h-Moll* noch eindeutig an klassischen Vorbildern orientiert und in einer spätromantischen Sprache verfasst ist, die den Einfluss von Richard Strauss, Hans Pfitzner und Max Reger erkennen lässt – wie zum Beispiel im ausgedehnten Fugenfinale des letzten Satzes – manifestiert sich in der *Sonate für Violoncello und Klavier* ein Duktus, der mit der Sprache des *Streichquartetts in h-Moll* nur noch wenig gemeinsam hat, das harmonische Vokabular rigoros – und mitunter unkonventionell – erweitert und stilistisch eher einen Einfluss Debussys nahelegt.

Ein klare Demarkationslinie trennt diese ersten beiden kammermusikalischen Werke Weills von den nächsten beiden, seinem *I. Streichquartett op. 8* und dem hier vorliegenden Liederzyklus *Frauentanz op. 10*. Dies macht sich sofort augenfällig bemerkbar, indem Weills autographe Notation insgesamt bedeutend klarer und unmissverständlicher wird, was auch darauf zurückzuführen ist, dass diese beiden Werke von der Universal Edition angenommen und veröffentlicht wurden und Weill sich deshalb bemühte, im Hinblick auf die Verwendung dieser Partituren als Stichvorlagen, seine Intentionen deutlicher zu fixieren. Aber auch stilistisch unterscheiden sich diese beiden Werke merklich vom *Streichquartett in h-Moll* sowie der *Sonate für Violoncello und Klavier*: sie weisen deutlich auf den Einfluss Ferruccio Busonis hin, dessen Idee einer „jungen Klassizität" einen beträchtlichen Eindruck auf Weill ausübte.

Weill begann mit der Arbeit am *Frauentanz op. 10* im Jahre 1923, unmittelbar nach der Vollendung des *I. Streichquartetts op. 8*. Was Weill dazu bewog, mittelalterliche Minnelieder (in zeitgenössischen Übersetzungen) zu vertonen, ist nicht bekannt; man kann vermuten, dass ähnliche Themen in Busonis Meisterklasse zur Diskussion kamen. Welche Textquelle Weill benutzte, ist bislang nicht geklärt; zum gegenwärtigen Zeitpunkt sind nur drei in den 1920er-Jahren im Druck erschienene Sammlungen bekannt, in denen man drei der sieben vertonten Dichtungen finden kann (wobei nur eine davon wörtlich mit dem Wortlaut im *Frauentanz* übereinstimmt); nähere Angaben dazu finden sich im Kritischen Bericht der Kritischen Edition.

Weill unternahm die Komposition des Werkes ohne die direkte Begutachtung seines verehrten Mentors Busoni. Aus Korrespondenz zwischen Philipp Jarnach, bei dem Weill zu dieser Zeit Kontrapunkt studierte, und Ferruccio Busoni, der sich gerade in Paris aufhielt, geht hervor, dass Busoni von Weills *Frauentanz* zunächst lediglich per Brief erfuhr; in einem Brief an Busoni vom 3. Oktober 1923 schrieb Jarnach: „Weill brachte mir seinen ‚Frauentanz', wovon ich entzückt bin. Das ist stellenweise sogar meisterlich." Dass Busoni den *Frauentanz* schließlich zur Einsicht erhielt und sehr schätzte, geht schon daraus hervor, dass er selbst den Klavierauszug des dritten Liedes „Ach wär mein Lieb ein Brünnlein kalt" verfasste; aus einem Brief Weills kann man entnehmen, dass Busoni sogar den ganzen Zyklus hatte einrichten wollen. Seine schwere Krankheit und Tod verhinderten dies.

Frauentanz wurde zum ersten Mal im Februar 1924 an der Preußischen Akademie der Künste in Berlin anlässlich eines Konzerts der Internationalen Gesellschaft für Neue Musik unter der Leitung von Fritz Stiedry aufgeführt; die Sopranistin war Nora Pisling-Boas. Die Pressestimmen waren insgesamt positiv. Die Drucklegung der Partitur und Stimmen bei der Universal Edition erfolgte zwischen Juni und September 1924, und ein Klavierauszug folgte 1925; Weill selbst bereitete diesen Klavierauszug vor (mit Ausnahme des von Busoni eingerichteten „Ach wär mein Lieb ein Brünnlein kalt"). Bis 1927 gehörte *Frauentanz* zu den am häufigsten aufgeführten Kompositionen Weills.

Während die erhaltenen autographen Quellen des *Streichquartetts in h-Moll* und der *Sonate für Violoncello und Klavier* einerseits geprägt sind durch ungenaue, flüchtige und häufig fehlerhafte Notation, andererseits als Quelle selbst nur unvollständig erhalten sind, zeichnen sich die Autographe des *I. Streichquartetts op. 8* sowie des *Frauentanzes op. 10* durch saubere, präzise Notation aus. Für den *Frauentanz* ist die Quellenlage unkompliziert.

In der zweiten Hälfte des Jahres 1923 schickte Weill sein erstes komplettes Autograph des *Frauentanzes* an die Universal Edition, die das Werk zur Veröffentlichung annahm. Anscheinend wurde von Weill eine neue Reinschrift angefordert, die dieser dann in der ersten Hälfte des Jahres 1924 ablieferte. Der von der Universal Edition im September 1924 veröffentlichten Partitur (zusammen mit den einzelnen Instrumentalstimmen) liegt Weills zweites Autograph als Stichvorlage zu Grunde. Weill selbst übernahm das Korrekturlesen der von der Universal Edition vorbereiteten Partitur und Stimmen.

Die hier vorliegende Ausgabe lehnt sich in sämtlichen Aspekten der Musik und des Textes an die von der Universal Edition 1924 veröffentlichte Partitur als Hauptquelle an. Diese repräsentiert das am weitesten fortgeschrittene Stadium des Werkes und kann darüber hinaus als von Weill autorisiert gelten, da dieser sie ja Korrektur gelesen hatte. Da Weills zweites Autograph als Stichvorlage diente, muss es gleichfalls als wichtige Quelle betrachtet werden: wo die Partitur der Universal Edition Fragen aufwirft, hat die hier vorliegende Ausgabe grundsätzlich Weills zweites Autograph hinzugezogen. In begrenztem Maße gilt dies auch für Weills erstes Autograph sowie die von der Universal Edition hergestellten Stimmen, da Weill diese ebenso vor ihrer Veröffentlichung einer Durchsicht unterzog. Eine detaillierte Besprechung der verschiedenen Quellen findet sich im Kritischen Bericht der Kritischen Edition.

Jürgen Selk
New York City, Juli 2005

Preface

Chamber music comprises only a relatively small portion of Weill's œuvre; it is represented by the *Streichquartett in h-Moll* (*String Quartet in B minor*), the *I. Streichquartett op. 8* (*String Quartet No. 1, op. 8*), the *Sonate für Violoncello und Klavier* (*Sonata for Violoncello and Piano*), the vocal-instrumental song cycle *Frauentanz op. 10* and the vocal-instrumental miniature *Ick sitze da – un esse Klops* (*I sit here – eating meatballs*). These works were published in 2004 in a Critical Edition edited by Wolfgang Rathert and Jürgen Selk, as part of the Kurt Weill Edition (Series II, Volume 1). The present practical edition of *Frauentanz op. 10* derives from the text of the Critical Edition.

Except for the *Meatball Song*, composed ca. 1925–1926, Weill wrote his remaining chamber music between 1918 and 1923. It reflects both Weill's development as a young composer as well as the external circumstances which influenced his progress, beginning with his studies at the Königlich Akademische Hochschule für Musik in Berlin under Engelbert Humperdinck (1918–1919), his brief tenure as conductor in Lüdenscheid (1919–1920), and his studies in Ferruccio Busoni's masterclass, beginning in 1921.

From the *String Quartet in B minor* (1918–1919), completed under Humperdinck's tutelage, to the *Sonata for Violoncello and Piano* (1919–1920), Weill's style undergoes a remarkable transformation. The *String Quartet in B minor* shows a clear orientation toward classical models; it is characterized by a late-romantic idiom that points toward the influence of Richard Strauss, Hans Pfitzner and Max Reger (as shown, for example, in the expansive fugue finale of the last movement). Weill's *Sonata for Violoncello and Piano*, on the other hand, signals a clear departure from this idiom; its expanded and unconventional harmonic vocabulary suggests instead the influence of Debussy.

A clear dividing line separates these first two works of Weill's chamber music from his next two contributions, the *String Quartet No. 1, op. 8* and the song cycle *Frauentanz op. 10*. One important difference is immediately apparent in the manuscripts: Weill's notation on the whole has become clearer and more precise. Universal Edition had accepted these two works for publication, and one suspects that for this reason, Weill was especially careful in his notation, knowing that his manuscripts would serve as engraver's models. But stylistically as well these two works differ significantly from his *String Quartet in B minor* and his *Sonata for Violoncello and Piano*; they point toward Ferruccio Busoni, whose vision of a 'new classicality' exerted a considerable influence on Weill.

Weill began work on *Frauentanz op. 10* in 1923, immediately upon completion of the *String Quartet No. 1, op. 8*. What motivated Weill to set medieval 'Minnelieder' (songs of courtly love) is unknown, but one can speculate that discussions in Busoni's masterclass might have revolved around similar topics. The sources of the texts have not yet been ascertained; at the present time only three printed collections, published in the 1920s, are known. They contain three of the seven poems, but only one of them coincides exactly with the text in *Frauentanz*; a more thorough discussion can be found in the Critical Report of the Critical Edition.

Weill undertook the composition of *Frauentanz* without the direct guidance of his revered mentor, Ferruccio Busoni. From correspondence between Philipp Jarnach, with whom Weill was studying counterpoint at the time, and Busoni, who was staying in Paris, we know that Busoni learned of Weill's *Frauentanz* at first only via letter. In a letter to Busoni from 3 October 1923, Jarnach wrote, 'Weill showed me his "Frauentanz", which delights me. In places it is truly a masterpiece.' Ultimately, Busoni did receive *Frauentanz* for review; he clearly liked the work, as evinced by the fact that he himself created a piano reduction of the third song 'Ach wär mein Lieb ein Brünnlein kalt'. We learn from one of Weill's letters that Busoni had intended to arrange the entire cycle; but his death on 27 July 1924 intervened.

Frauentanz was first performed in February 1924 at the Preußische Akademie der Künste in Berlin at a concert of the Internationale Gesellschaft für Neue Musik, under the direction of Fritz Stiedry; the soprano was Nora Pisling-Boas. Press reviews on the whole were positive. Universal Edition published score and parts between June and September 1924, and the piano-vocal score in 1925; Weill himself had prepared the piano-vocal score (except for 'Ach wär mein Lieb ein Brünnlein kalt', where he retained Busoni's arrangement). Until 1927, *Frauentanz* remained one of Weill's most frequently performed compositions.

Whereas the extant autograph sources of the *String Quartet in B minor* and the *Sonata for Violoncello and Piano* are characterized by imprecise, hasty and often faulty notation, the autographs of the *String Quartet No. 1, op. 8* and *Frauentanz op. 10* are notated cleanly and precisely. For *Frauentanz*, the disposition of the sources is uncomplicated.

Weill submitted a first autograph fair copy of *Frauentanz* to Universal Edition, probably in the second half of 1923. Universal Edition accepted the work but, for the purposes of engraving, may have requested an improved fair copy from Weill. The composer then submitted a second autograph fair copy, most likely in the first half of 1924. The score as published by Universal Edition in September 1924 (together with instrumental parts) was produced on the basis of Weill's second autograph. Weill himself undertook the proofreading of the engraved full score and parts.

The present edition privileges the engraved score, published by Universal Edition in 1924, as the main source for all aspects of music and text. The 1924 publication represents the most advanced state of the work and can be regarded as having been authorized by Weill, as he himself had proofread it. As Weill's second autograph was used as the engraver's model, it likewise constitutes an important source. Where the evidence in the published score raises questions, the second autograph was consulted for possible alternatives, as were the first autograph and the engraved parts. The latter two sources offer significant insight as well because of Weill's close involvement with them. A detailed description of the various sources can be found in the Critical Report of the Critical Edition.

Jürgen Selk
New York City, July 2005

Sopran	Soprano
Flöte	Flute
Bratsche	Viola
Klarinette in B	Clarinet in B♭
Horn in F	Horn in F
Fagott	Bassoon

Nelly Frank gewidmet

Frauentanz
Sieben Gedichte des Mittelalters
op. 10 (1923/1924)

I

Kurt Weill
(1900–1950)

Andantino, quasi Tempo di Menuetto

European American Music Corporation EA 848S
Universal Edition UE 33081

winter-lan-ge Nacht mit Freu-den wohl emp-fan-gen, ich und ein Rit-ter

wohl-be-dacht, sein Wil-le ist er-gan-gen.

poco rall. a tempo

Wie wir es bei-de___ uns ge-dacht, so hat ers

molto espr.

(Dietmar von Aiste.)

II

Allegro non troppo

Gesang
Klarinette in B
Horn in F
Fagott

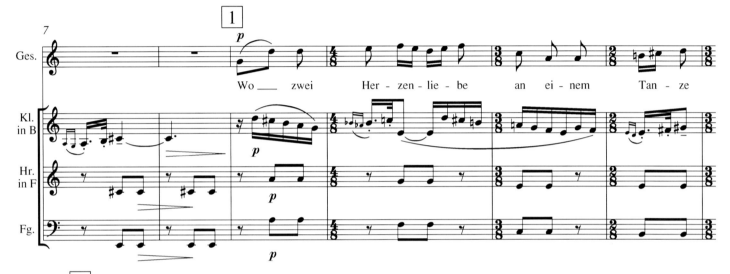

7

Wo ___ zwei Her - zen - lie - be an ei - nem Tan - ze

13

gan, sie las - sent ihr Äu - ge - lin schie - ßen,

19

sie se - hent ein - an - der ___ an.

(Dichter unbekannt.)

III

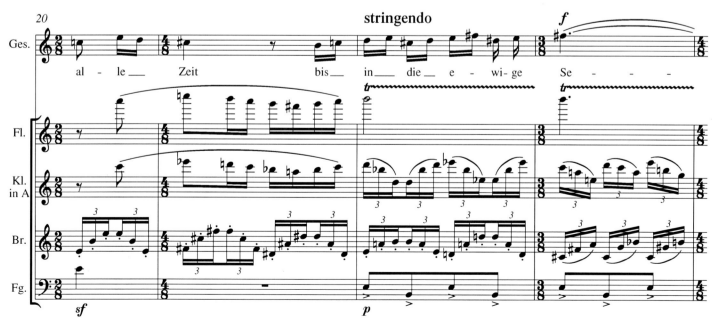

(Dichter unbekannt.)

IV

Tranquillo e molto piano

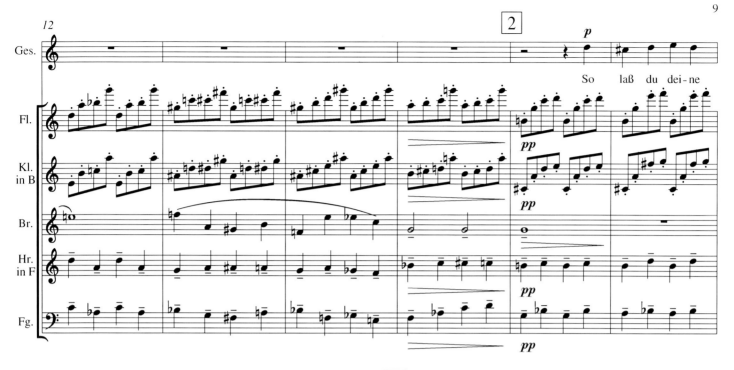

(Der von Kürenberg.)

V

(Herzog Johann von Brabant.)

VI

(Dichter unbekannt.)

VII

(Dichter unbekannt.)

SEVEN POEMS FROM THE MIDDLE AGES

I

With joy did we bid welcome to
The lengthy winter's night
I and an admirable knight,
His will has fled from him.

His joy and mine did he foretell
In coming to an end
With certain gladness and much love
He's how I'd have him be.

II

As two loving hearts
Began a dance
Like arrows darted forth their glance
They gazed at one another.
Like arrows darted forth their glance
As if they had no cares,
In silent yearning do they think
Oh, to lie near to thee.

III

Oh, were my love a spring so cool
Which bubbled from a stone,
If I were then the deep green woods
I'd drink it thirstily,
It should flow on unendingly
And totally engulf me,
Yesterday, now, forevermore,
Eternally in ecstasy.

IV

This star in the dark heavens
See, veiled, how it does hide,
Do likewise, lovely lady,
If ever you see me.
And if your eye should wander
Upon another man,
Yet nobody can fathom
Just what we two have shared.

Translated by George Sturm

V

On a morning fair in May
Did I early arise,
In a garden in bloom
Did I go to play,
And there I found three maidens,
One started to sing
The other one too
Singing "harbalorifa".

When I saw the lovely leaves
In the garden in bloom
And I heard the dulcet sound
Of the maidens fine,
My heart quickened so
That I sang along: "harbalorifa".

Then I greeted the very fairest
Among the maidens three,
I slid my arm around her waist
And wanted then
To kiss her on the lips
When she spoke: "Don't touch,
Don't touch me, harbalorifa."

VI

I think that I have mourned enough
We should now to the meadow go
And many lovers' games there play
While watching the fair flowers grow.

I tell to thee, I tell you true,
Come, love, with me, oh do.

Sweet love, wouldst thou my lover be
And make for me a wreath of flowers
Which any man would proudly wear
While showing girls his magic powers.

I tell to thee. etc.

VII

I sleep, I wake, I walk, I stand,
My being have you captured,
I seem to see thee constantly
My heart have you enraptured.

How wondrous fair your features are,
Gone is my relaxation
On earth and all creation.